MIKE THOMPSON 12/01

MOTOONS

A COLLECTION OF POLITICAL CARTOONS BY

MIKE THOMPSON

Detroit Free Press

Detroit Free Press

600 W. Fort
Detroit, Mich. 48226
www.freep.com

Other recent books by the Free Press:

Ernie Harwell	The Detroit Almanac	Heart Smart Kids Cookbook
State of Glory	Corner to Copa	The Corner
Century of Champions	PC@Home	Yaklennium
Believe!	Stanleytown	

To order any of these titles, please call 800-245-5082 or go to **www.freep.com/bookstore**
To subscribe to the Free Press, call 800-395-3300

Motoons
ISBN 0-937247-37-5
$9.95

Mike Thompson's daily editorial cartoons can be viewed in color
on the Internet at **www.freep.com/index/thompson.htm**

Production, design and copy editing: Gerald Skora
Back cover photography: Free Press chief photographer J. Kyle Keener
Editorial page editor: Ron Dzwonkowski
Associate editorial page editor: Becca Rothschild
Project coordinator: Dave Robinson
Technical and design assistance: A.J. Hartley, Steve Dorsey
Special assistance: Connie Thompson, Barbara Arrigo, Linda McCraith

Introduction

L ate in the afternoon of any given day, you'll find Mike Thompson hunched low over the wide drawing table that pretty well fills his office in a corner of the editorial department of the Detroit Free Press.

Some people work with their nose to the grindstone. Mike's nose is practically touching the cardboard mat where his latest idea is taking shape. Lost in concentration, his fingers stained with black ink, Mike appears oblivious to his office temperature, which is always too hot or too cold, to the TV that is constantly blaring news, and to the inquisitive face of his daughter looking up from the screen saver of his computer.

But Mike is zeroing in on a target. Perhaps a certain rotund governor, a jug-eared president in short pants, an off-balance foreign dictator, or maybe America's lust for ever-larger SUVs.

It's one thing to have an opinion, another to explain it in words that make sense. Try drawing what you think to illustrate your point.

That's what Mike Thompson does for the Free Press. He is a visual columnist, presenting his view of the world in words and art that can be outrageous, humorous, poignant and provocative — all in the same day, depending how readers see it.

Mike's artwork is the dominant image on the Free Press editorial page five days a week, more often when developments warrant, such as the Sept. 11 terrorist attacks or the 2000 election debacle in Florida.

Mike swings from the left, but he doesn't play favorites, taking aim at hypocrisy wherever he sees it and ridiculing American foibles wherever they appear.

Mike came to the Free Press in November 1998 from Springfield, Ill., where he spent eight years drawing cartoons for Copley Newspapers in the Prairie State.

A native of Minnesota, Mike, 37, is the second oldest of four children. Dad was an art professor at the University of Minnesota and an art museum curator, and Mom was an English teacher, which may explain Mike's penchant for self-expression in art *and* words.

Mike has been drawing as long as he can remember — going back to sketches of his teachers in school, not all of which were appreciated. He could have pursued a conventional career in art, but says, "I really didn't want to starve."

Mike's first cartoons were published in the student paper at Washburn High School in south Minneapolis. Mike went on to the University of Wisconsin at Milwaukee, where he drew well enough for the campus paper to earn the Charles Schulz Award from the Scripps Howard Foundation as America's outstanding young cartoonist.

That led to two years of regular work for the Milwaukee Journal and the Locher Award from the American Association of Editorial Cartoonists. From there, Mike accepted a job at the St. Louis Sun, which folded after a year. That proved to be a life-changing experience, because Mike met his wife, Connie, in St. Louis.

Since joining the Free Press, Mike has been recognized by both the National Press Foundation and the Society of Professional Journalists as the nation's outstanding editorial cartoonist.

You might think all this would go to his head. But that head is too full of ideas just waiting for Mike's gifted hand to bring them to life.

— **Ron Dzwonkowski**
Editor, Free Press Editorial Page

Michigan

The Nation

The World

Life in America

Sports

"WE'RE UP NORTH, Y'KNOW, JUST GETTING AWAY FROM IT ALL..."

HIGH CULTURE MEETS HOCKEYTOWN

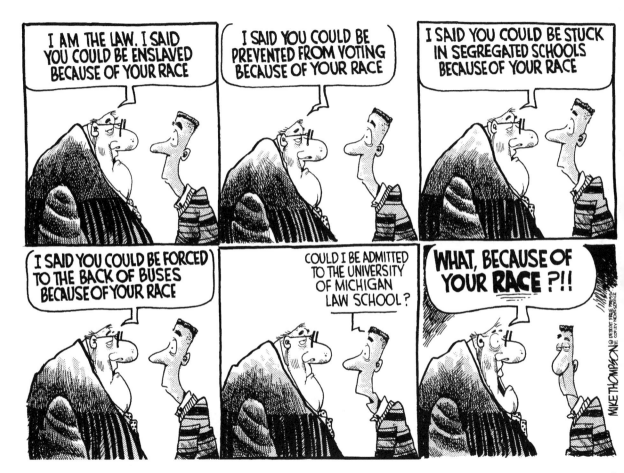

3

"I DIDN'T KNOW A CHILD'S LIFE HAD VALUE"

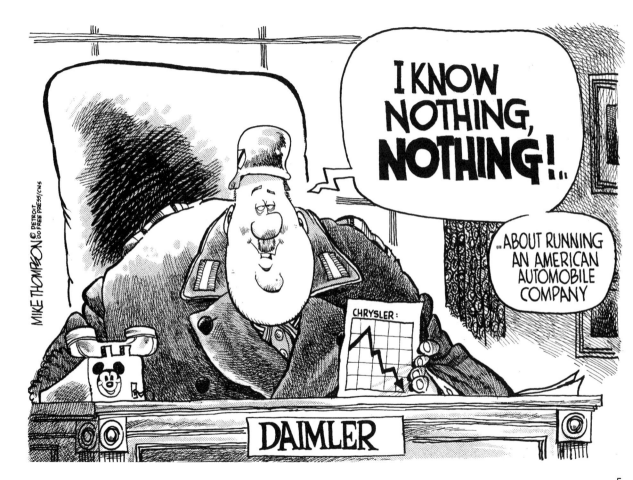

6

7

Unscheduled Maintenance

9

Same ol' Archer

11

12

13

15

Had the victim been white

17

FIELD OF PIPE DREAMS

19

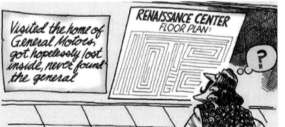

Discovered an (Aztec?) pyramid, the kind with tall, steep steps leading up to a temple where locals worship their Gods.

I found a Roman Coliseum where gladiators don't get slaughtered, tigers do. Think I'll stay awhile and watch the carnage...

...there's plenty of empty seats!

The local vegetation is unusual. One orange plant seems to pop up everywhere.

Beautiful cement riverwalk good for taking a stroll... ...Bad for pitching a tent!

"MEAP, MEAP!"

23

24

25

26

27

28

"PROBLEM? WHAT PROBLEM?"

30

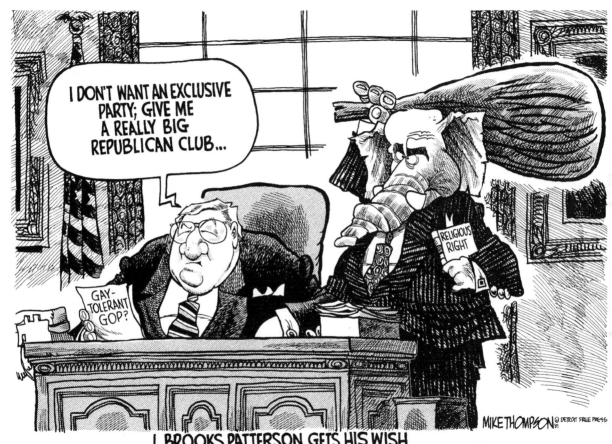

L. BROOKS PATTERSON GETS HIS WISH

33

34

35

36

37

GOVERNOR ENGLER
And His Triplets

YOUNG • MARKMAN • TAYLOR

MIKE THOMPSON / DETROIT FREE PRESS

38

39

40

Thanks to the LAME-DUCK LEGISLATURE, MICHIGAN will HAVE...

... MORE MOURNING DOVES

... AND MORE MOURNING HUMANS.

42

"MAYBE THE SAYING SHOULD GO: 'NEVER WATCH SAUSAGES OR **PLEA DEALS** BEING MADE.'"

43

44

45

46

47

The Nation

... Gave proof through the night that our flag was still there.

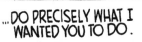

50

THE ACME INSURANCE COMPANY
LIFE - HOME - AUTO

Dear Mr. Osama bin Laden:

We regret to inform you that we've abruptly
canceled your life insurance policy.

Sincerely,

Ben Niceknowinya,
Agent

MIKE THOMPSON © DETROIT FREE PRESS/COPLEY NEWS SERVICE

51

STOCK REPORT

52

53

55

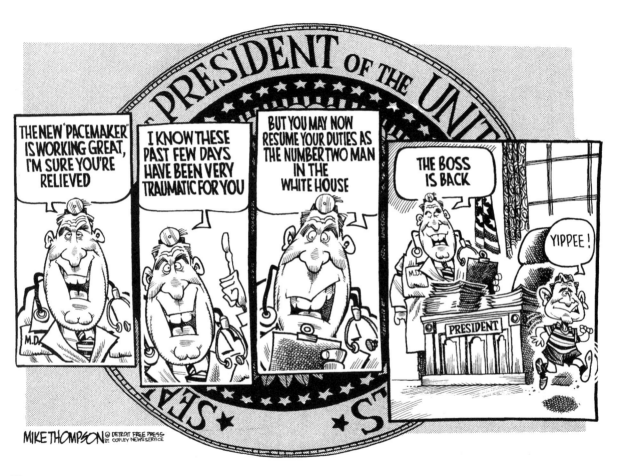

56

DÉJÀ VOODOO

57

59

61

63

64

65

66

69

The George W. Bush
Social Security
LOCKBOX

ATM

MIKE THOMPSON @ DETROIT FREE PRESS
'01 COPLEY NEWS SERVICE

70

71

72

Stem Cell Research: The First Mutation

73

74

76

77

MIKE THOMPSON
POPULAR VOTE
PRESIDENTIAL ELECTION
ELECTORAL VOTE
You're right, it is a hell of a way to run a railroad

"THINK SECRETARY OF STATE HARRIS IS ACTING A BIT TOO PARTISAN?."

The Torch is Passed

82

83

84

85

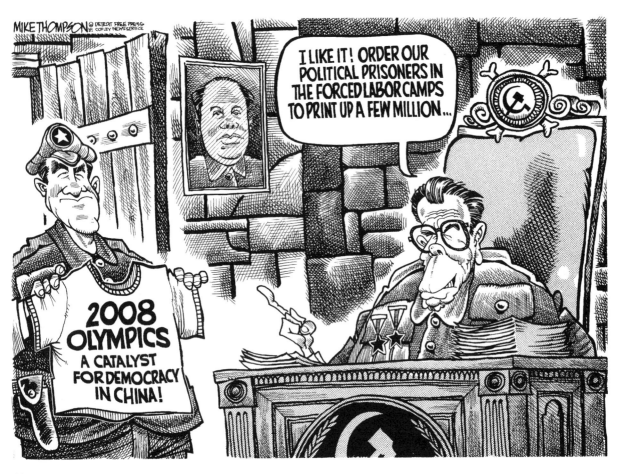

86

SUDDENLY, AN AMERICAN MILITARY RESPONSE TO AN INVASION BY CHINA WAS NO LONGER IN DOUBT

89

"BUSH?.. BUSH?.. WASN'T YOUR FATHER A PUPIL OF MINE?.."

91

94

95

98

99

100

101

Life in America

104

105

106

107

108

109

111

112

113

"DOES THE TERM 'PROFESSIONAL WRESTLING REFEREE' COME TO MIND?.."

"REMIND ME WHY THEY'RE CONSIDERED THE MORE EVOLVED SPECIES"

115

"I'D RATHER YOU DIDN'T... BUT IF YOU MUST DRIVE TO THE SUBURBS, KEEP YOUR DOORS LOCKED AND STAY OFF THE SIDE STREETS."

117

Dear President Bush,
  Thank you for your plan to test all students. The tests are very useful...

119

BARBIE AT 40, IF SHE WERE REAL

120

HealthRisks Associated with Cell Phone Usage:

BRAIN TUMORS:

HARMFUL DOSES OF RADIATION:

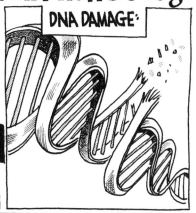

DNA DAMAGE:

MULTIPLE CUTS AND BRUISES:

122

123

Dennis Tito, space tourist

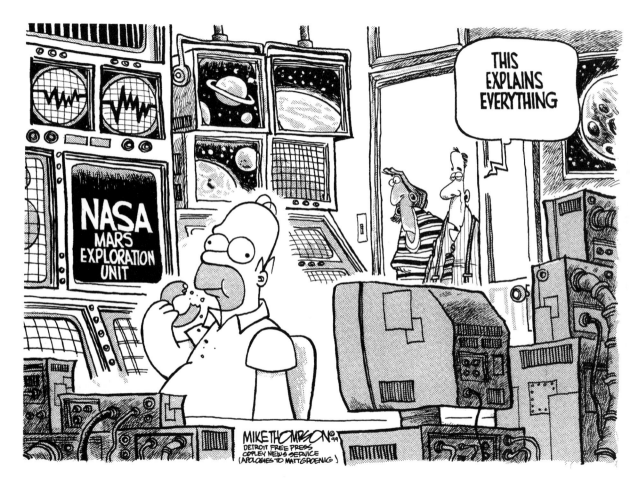

125

126

127

In a perfect world

129

(CON) ARTIST OF THE YEAR PRESENTATION

131

Sports

Baseball at the Corner 1896-1999

"TIGERS HIGHLIGHTS UP NEXT ...PLEASE STAY TUNED ANYWAY..."

135

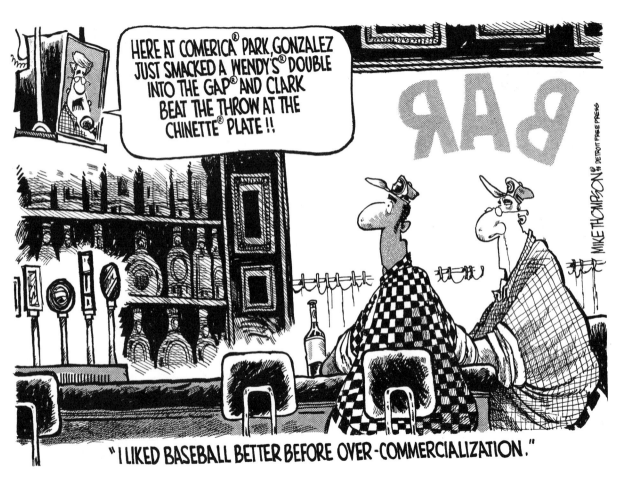

136

137

138

139

140

141

MIKE THOMPSON'S PLAYOFF FEVER SKETCHBOOK

NICE OF GOVERNOR ENGLER TO LEND HIS JERSEY

TICKETS TO THE FIRST HOME GAME OF THE SECOND ROUND:

$160

TWO BEERS AND A LARGE POPCORN:

$17

SEEING THE 'INVINCIBLE' PATRICK ROY GO DOWN IN FLAMES:

PRICELESS

We offer 36-month financing at 12-percent interest with 10 percent down.

Last time I buy a beer at the Joe

142

144

MISSION: IMPROBABLE

145

Super Bowl viewing SIGNALS:

NO, I WON'T FETCH YOU A BEER, HONEY

GREG GUMBEL'S DOING THE PLAY-BY-PLAY

'N SYNC IS PERFORMING AT HALFTIME!

THINKING A GAME BETWEEN TWO DEFENSE-ORIENTED TEAMS WILL BE ENTERTAINING

SERVED RED WINE TO SUPER BOWL PARTY GUESTS IN HOME WITH WHITE CARPETING

COMMERCIALS ARE OVER, GAME'S BACK ON

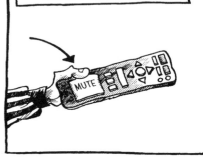

MIKE THOMPSON © DETROIT FREE PRESS

146

148

149

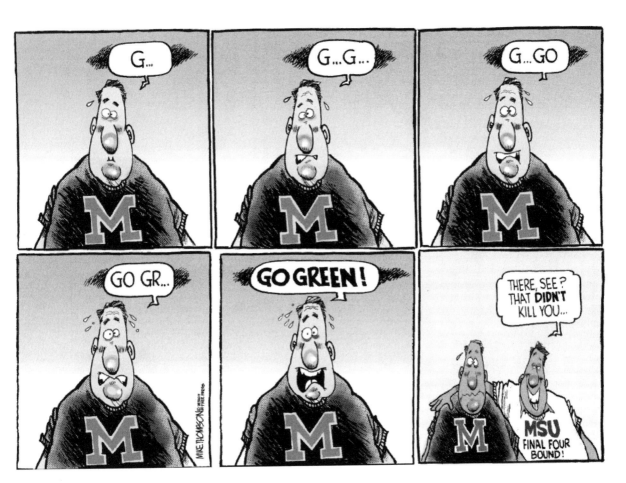

150

151